HOW TO WRITE

A Christian Writer's Guide

MIRIAM ADENEY

REGENT COLLEGE
REPRINT

Copyright © Miriam Adeney

First published 1972 by
Asia Christian Communications Fellowship.

North American edition published with permission
by Regent Bookstore, 1994.
5800 University Boulevard, Vancouver B.C. V6T 2E4, Canada

Second printing, 1994   Third printing, 1995

Library of Congress Cataloguing in Publication Data

ADENEY, MIRIAM.
  How to Write/ Miriam Adeney. (1945-)
    p. cm.

  1. Authoriship -- Handbooks, manuals, etc.
  II. Title
PN145.A268   1994

ISBN 1-57383-028-3

CONTENTS

1. WHY WRITE?

When Daniel was a young man, the imperialistic empire of the Chaldeans colonized Judah, and Judah became a puppet nation.

Nebuchadnezzar, the Chaldean emperor, was no fool. His policies were positive, developmental, integrative, and unafraid—signs of a great ruler. He respected worthy people of every race. So when he conquered a nation, he gathered up its most promising young people and sent them to his capital—like sending people to London or Peking or Washington. There they learned the Chaldean language and all the science of the Chaldeans. When they were graduated, they were placed in prestigious positions in the Chaldean bureaucracy. By doing this, Nebuchadnezzar bought the loyalty of those who were most capable of leading a revolution in every land that he colonized.

When the Chaldeans conquered Judah, Daniel was among the bright young men marched off to Babylon. There he distinguished himself by his wisdom, by his reputation for standing up for his convictions, and by his attractive personality—as those in charge of the boys could not help loving Daniel. You can find all this in the book of Daniel in the Old Testament.

Then something dramatic erupted. Nebuchadnezzar had a dream—and he forgot what it was. In those days dreams were a chief source of information, instead of computers and data banks. But Nebuchadnezar forgot this dream—a tragedy as great as losing vital secret documents.

So he was frantic. He called in his magicians, the intelligentsia of the day, and demanded that they tell him his dream and its meaning. Of course they were shocked. This was beyond the range of their competency, they protested. But Nebuchadnezzar was not persuaded. What use are religious specialists in a bureaucracy if they can't help in a crisis? He suspected featherbedding. So he decided to exterminate the whole brain trust and get a new one.

The next thing Daniel knew, he was on the way to the firing squad. "What's this all about?" he asked. When he found out, he decided it was time to gamble on God. So he stepped out and volunteered to become a bridge between the condemned and the condemner. He announced that if the king would give him a little time, he would discover not only the meaning of the dream, but the dream itself.

Then he got down to business. There was no time to mimeograph a prayer letter. But he contacted the local people of God, and they dropped what they were doing. It wasn't an individualistic effort. Each gave what he had— one his parapsychological ability to perceive the unknown, the others their time and energies in serious prayer support.

And, very simply we are told, "Then the secret was revealed to Daniel in a night vision."

What relief! What a put-down to the others in the brain trust. And what anticipation—because Daniel was scheduled for an immediate conference with Nebuchadnezzar. That meant getting his pants pressed, having his finger nails manicured, and checking out the latest revisions in court etiquette.

But Daniel also made time for something else. Before all the flurry began, he sat down and composed a poem–a vibrating verse in the balanced stanzas of Hebrew poetry.

Now this was not the result of a course in Christian writing. Daniel had not scheduled writing as one of his top priorities for the year. No, this was just **the spontaneous response of an educated person in the course of a living relationship with God.**

A lot of the Hebrew poetry sprouted up like this—like the poems of Miriam and Hannah and Mary.

Why should you get involved in Christian writing? "I'd love to, but I have no time," you may say. Schedules and specializations may compartmentalize your life for efficiency.

But wouldn't it be rewarding to occasionally sit down and scribble out an unplanned response to God when he has interacted with you in a crisis? This was why some biblical authors wrote.

Others wrote because they felt a compulsion to record what God was doing. These journalists turned out the prosy historical sections of the Bible. They didn't get stirred up at a writers' conference. They weren't commissioned by a mission organization to write a book. But as distinct individuals they felt compelled to sit down and record contemporary local dealings of God with man.

They nailed down biographies, histories, and social commentaries. As we read these today, they drive home to us the nature of man and the nature of God. We discover that even the men who know God best turn selfish again and again. Yet as we study these diverse personalities in various cultures who have known God—this cloud of witnesses extending over the centuries—we see unmistakably what they are corporately witnessing to: the faithfulness of God.

Does God interact with man today? Do you personally know anybody whom God has helped? If you do, consider recording this episode which illustrates another facet of God's dealings with man. Advertise the fact that God is not only the God of Israel or England or the U.S., but that He is also alive among your own people. Why leave your chapter of church history unrecorded?

Other biblical writers were burdened to speak to some problem pressing on the people of God. This provoked many of the New Testament epistles. God gives writers their gift of expression so that they will edify his body, the church—so that we can all grow up in Christ together, able to speak the truth in love.

What problems do you see in your church? Division over personalities? Fear of non-Christians? Fear of the future? Materialism? Preoccupation with externals? Laziness and poor use of time? Ignorance of the Scriptures? A generation gap? Write to these needs.

"But the mass media is so impersonal!" you may protest. "How can I write to these needs when I cannot see the readers?"

Look at the book of Colossians. It is a specific book, and a warm one. In Col. 2:1, the apostle Paul tells the Colossian Christians he wishes they knew what a huge conflict he feels inside for them. Later he writes, "Though I am absent in the flesh, yet I am with you in the spirit, joying and beholding your order, and the steadfastness of your faith in Christ." But he had never met the Colossians! He was like today's Christian writer, burdened for the needs of an unseen and unmet audience.

Yet these readers were no faceless mass for Paul. No, he had boned up on their background, their progress, and their current conditions. By now he felt profound empathy with them. After painstaking, loving study of his readers, Paul reached powerfully across the miles to help this section of Christ's Church—through writing.

The biblical men also spoke to restless people about the life available in Jesus Christ. Look at your own people. Look at the grimy men following their buffaloes through the rice fields, their wives haggling over fish in the market, their children spelling out the words in the comic books. Look at the young men lounging over pornographic magazines on the corner, the aggressive decision-makers in the skyscrapers, the sophisticates in the radio studios and advertising agencies. Look at the Church straggling across your nation. Then look at the mass media. Where is the message of Jesus Christ? Where is the good news for the simple young girl who comes with dreams and ideals to the city? Where is hope for the frustrated and grasping young man?

Yes, we must communicate.

But publishing programs are expensive. They draw a lot of Christian workers away from direct evangelism and church planting. They are slower than preaching, less personal than individual witnessing. In fact they can grab our attention until we're concerned about piling up statistics–40,000 tracts distributed in a crusade—more than we are concerned about patient love for our neighbors. Writers can so easily become religious technicians–Marthas rather than Marys.

So why bother with Christian writing? Why not just preach, teach, and do personal evangelism?

Writing has some special strengths. **You can reach large numbers of people simultaneously through printed matter.** At the University of the Philippines, a few years aqo, Christian students sold almost five thousand copies of an evangelistic newspaper, which resulted in many Bible studies and subsequent conversions. It would have taken much longer to reach all these people with the gospel through friendship and small group discussions.

According to a recent survey, some of the fastest growing churches in Malaysia rely primarily on postal and radio Bible courses for their evangelism.

Many individuals all over the world have encountered and committed themselves to their Savior through books, tracts, and especially through the Bible. How do you discover these receptive people? You broadcast the news widely so that those who are thirsty will learn where the Living Water is. For this mass announcement, you need mass communication.

A printed message can be kept, reread, and studied. People may forget what you say about Christ—or they may remember only part, and twist the meaning. But if the message is in black and white in front of them, they can study it at their leisure, without being able to ignore the parts they would rather not remember. The whole thing stays with them.

A printed message can penetrate privately. The reader does not have to keep up his defenses as he might if someone were sharing the gospel with him face to face. He can explore his soul with complete honesty in the light of the message he is reading.

A meaty book can feed the hungry spirit for hours or even days. It can give him massive doses of information, equal to dozens of sermons and counselling sessions.

A printed message is ideal for exact explanation of what Christians believe and how this differs from, say, the teachings of Islam or the Jehovah's Witnesses or local religions. Somewhere in our evangelism we need to be able to give extensive, logical explanation of the hope that is in us. TV and radio can grab attention in the mainstream of life. Personal evangelists can interact back and forth with the specific questions of individuals. But all communication specialists agree that printed matter is best for communicating information in explicit detail.

A Christian periodical which comes out regularly shows that there is a reference group, a circle of identity and friendship, made up of diverse individual Christians. This is a tremendous encouragement to the sincere inquirer as he becomes aware of the variety of those who believe in Christ, as well as of their corporate strength and warmth. Obviously the publishing program should not be run by foreigners. Nor should the writers try to remain inconspicuous. Readers need to identify the message with placeable people if they are to see its relevance to their real lives.

A Christian article can get the gospel into the mass media as an ideological alternative. There is no question that mass media influence people. Leaders especially expect mass media to keep them informed about the most important facts of life.

What life alternatives do mass media present? They say you can find the good life through material success (just listen to the advertisements !). Or in romantic love and a warm family. In your traditional religion. In Marxism. Or in a counter-culture. Or you can decide life has no meaning: it is just a commodity you measure out in bus rides.

Are there any others alternatives? Christian writing should be popping out regulary to insist that the ideological options are not complete unless the gospel of Jesus Christ is also considered. Why do so many people lose their faith when they move to the city and become educated? Could it be because Christianity is not presented in urban thought patterns through the mass media? Could it be because Christianity seems to be concerned only for the unsophisticated?

As well as producing Christian publications, then, we must also buy time on secular radio stations, write letters to the editors of our daily newspapers, and publish articles in our national weekly women's magazines and monthly youth periodicals and journals of public opinion

Finally, **printed matter can penetrate closed countries** with the good news of Christ. If well-written and designed, these materials can communicate without any foreign appearance or accent.

These are the strengths of Christian writing. God's Word does not return to Him void. It is quick and powerful, and pierces deep into a man.

But do not become smug about Christian writing. Literature has no magic. And you can write or distribute Christian literature in a careless or impersonal spirit that almost blasphemes the real word of God. Your life can focus on production more than on holiness. You can be motivated by a selfish thirst for statistics more than by a love for whole people. Power corrupts. Writing to several thousand people is power. You can become "cool" about lost human beings.

How different this is from the biblical authors! They wrote to respond to God, to record what God was doing or to meet needs among Christians or non-Christians. Let us follow them. Is God doing something that you should respond to or record? Is there a need that you should speak to? This is our challenge as we continue in the biblical tradition.

2.   WHO WILL WRITE?

Who are Asia's Christian writers? In every race, in every social class, there are men and women who should be reflecting the lives of their people in writing. Who are they?

People who love words. According to anthropologists, man is not primarily distinguished from animals by his reasoning power but by his ability to create words. Words are tools of power, moving the mind. They are also tools of beauty, moving the heart. Consider these:

Who has measured the waters in the hollow of his hand, and marked off the heavens with a span, enclosed the dust of the earth in a measure, and weighed the mountains in scales, and the hills in a balance?

Who has directed the Spirit of the Lord, or as his counsellor has instructed Him ? [1]

Arise, my love, my fair one, and come away.
For lo, the winter is past, the rain is over and gone. The flowers appear on the earth, the time of singing has come, and the voice of the turtledove is heard in our land. The fig tree puts forth its figs, and the vines are in blossom.
They give forth fragrance.
Arise, my love, my fair one, and come away. [2]

We fly out (of Russia). What a relief ....

Below, the clouds are closing over the plain of dead armies, the white birches bare, womanlike trees shivering in the snow.

Europe soon, and the neon signs brightening the avenue, blazing shop windows full of beautiful things again, plenty. Plenty . . . and the blacks and the students hoisting strange flags on the statues, the magazines announcing revolution in five color photos, cities on fire beside the green golf course, more bombs dropped on one Vietnam than on the whole earth in World War 11, stereophonic sound in new U.S. cars . . . In Chicago soon Allen Ginsberg will be humming his Ooommm to the enraged and astounded cops. The plane's compass steadily hangs on the "W", and thank God. But which way is man? Anywhere? [3]

The beauty of these words stretches across time and space. But is there not a Christian sprung from your own soil who is in love with words today? A man who can give voice to the longings and delights of your people in rhythm, imagery, phrases with contrast, and words that are fresh?

A good writer envisions more intensity than he can ever express. "Human language is like a cracked kettle on which we beat out tunes for bears to dance to, when all the time we are longing to move the stars to pity," said Flaubert. So the writer sweats and scrawls and scratches out all his life in an unending, maddening but liberating struggle to find the exact word.

People who love ideas. Words do not have power in themselves, but as vehicles for ideas. And "nothing is as powerful as an idea whose time has come." But an uncommunicated idea dies. The ideas of a silent majority are useless. Ideas need writers.

Have you done some hard thinking about life today? Do you have ideas on how a person can be vitally involved in his job, a real friend to his co-workers, and yet be holy? How can we creatively combat the dullness of routine work and the dinginess of much city life? Do you have counsel for single girls who are getting older and lonelier? What about the strains between Christ's call and family obligations? Can you help the marriages that are being eroded by nagging or by neglect? How much freedom should young people expect?

On a broader scale, do you look at the things that are happening to your country as any atheist would, or do you try to see the hand of God in current events? Can you comment biblically on your national health program, your educational system, your country's economic plans, nationalism, the use of natural resources, and what your country is doing for the poor?

Have you pondered such questions? People need guidance in these dilemmas—even if it is not expressed in beautiful words. In fact, when an issue is raging, the rough writer with workable ideas is more valuable than the perfect stylist.

To increase the worth of your ideas, broaden your experience. A great writer is like an iceberg—eighty per cent is below the surface, according to novelist Ernest Hemingway. So read widely: it will keep your mind well stocked. Be awake to issues covered in the press or rumbling in the coffee shops. Develop opinions, and practice expressing them. Study the Bible regularly in search of principles which can be applied to life. Brush elbows with Christians and non-Christians, seeing them as they actually are, feeling their crises. Observe what is going on in the house next door. Be curious about details, and note and remember little things that you see and hear and feel.

God gives us insight in varying degrees. Just as you are a steward of your money and talents, so you are a steward of your insight and ideas. You are responsible to spread them as widely as they will be helpful.

Why has God allowed you to go through confusing, shameful, painful, lonely experiences? Perhaps He wants to mellow your insight into something of broader scope and more lasting value. Let Him.

In your ideals, you should hunger for God's holiness to be expressed in society. But in your suggestions you must be more realistic than perfectionistic. "We live in a sinful, fallen world, and it will be like this until Jesus comes again, A democracy where biblical Christians are in the minority may be a long way from God's absolute standard, but it may be the best we can get. We will often have to choose between a lesser and a greater evil, as between divorce on one hand and abandoned wives and suffering concubines on the other. Many would rather opt out than make these difficult choices. But that is not an honest alternative for the faithful Christian."[4]

A writer who loves ideas will avoid becoming a propagandist for any organization. With humility but also with stubborn conviction, he will praise or criticize every group on the basis of what he observes. Writers are society's watchdogs, warning people of their faults, helping citizens maintain surveillance for weaknesses in their systems. Writers "have a lover's quarrel with the world." Christians are inherently anti-establishment, "lights in a dark place." So Christian writers must be doubly willing to stand alone with their ideas. Do you write your own vision, or do you write what people hire you to say?

People who love people. "If I speak with the tongues of men and of angels, but have not love, I am a noisy gong or a clanging cymbal." Many students argue eloquently for mankind, but have little love for their own families and neighbors. Christian writers cannot be just "idea men." We must be men who delight in the variety of mankind and the loveliness of each man made in the image of God, and who ache over every man's tragedies and foolishness.

Are people human? A sociologist who studied the farmers of the Northwest U.S.A. found that these farmers perceived reality in three categories (1) scenery; (2) machinery and other useful things; and (3) people. And unconsciously these farmers viewed American Indians more as scenery than as people—and Mexican laborers primarily as useful things! Sometimes, we must admit, as we jostle with thousands, we are no more aware of these souls for whom Christ died than we are of the telephone poles that we pass on the street.

But as Christian writers we must force ourselves to see even strangers as human beings, with hopes and troubles and a worth as intense as our own.

People have economic and political needs, and writers should crusade about these. But let us not see certain groups only as objects needing help. Let us not see only their poverty. Even amid squalor and disorganized families and periodic drunkenness and stabbings, there is family warmth and children's games and gaiety and dancing and loving sacrifice. The needy still have some pride.

Even a person who does not accomplish anything has value for the writer. "If a lamb should die in May, before it had reproduced itself, or contributed to the development of the species, or provided a fleece for the market, still the fact that it frisked and frolicked in the spring is in one sense an end in itself, and in another sense a thing that tends to the glory of God."[5]

People who love the old ways. A writer needs roots in the past. Your people's identity is bound up with the past. Certain historic wars and conquests, certain trading relationships with other nations, certain mountain ranges and seas, certain typhoons and droughts, certain kin ties and village patterns, certain old customs and courtesies have helped make your people what they are today. Though you may be an advocate of modern progress, you must also love the old traditions if you are to write about your people with depth.

People who love the new ways. On the outskirts of the city the wind ripples the fields of green rice. The laborers' brown muscles are coated with sweat. Girls toss rice in the air from flat baskets. Vendors' calls ring through the streets. Outside the cool temple, a cock arches to crow. Life continues as it has for centuries. Yet there are also modern young couples who want to live independently. More young boys are taking drugs and more young girls are becoming "hostesses." More people are leaving the green rice fields for the hot, hard city, and the buses are bursting with bodies. Ph. D.'s and Boeing 747's and computers and new industries are arriving.

As a writer, you cannot stay in the past. You cannot keep writing about the traditional family pattern if the young people are already rejecting it in favor of smaller, freer families. You must take a clear look at where your people are going. Then you must step out in front to guide them. Of course you don't have all the answers. But if someone doesn't guide your people, they will slide forward helplessly without direction. Change is sure to come. Are you preparing your people for it?

People who love the Word of God. As old and new value systems collide, how can you choose the right way? You need guidance from outside your culture. Fortunately, a guidebook is available in the Word of God—the record of God's attitudes to man's affairs for thousands of years. These attitudes yield principles that you can apply to situations confronting your society now.

People who love God. If you have a living, personal relationship with God through Christ, then spend time with Him every day. The Holy Spirit will gather together stray thoughts in your subconscious mind and will present you with fresh creative insights, saving you hours of mental struggle.

Time with God also reminds you that you must make yourself a "living sacrifice" each day. As you do this, your personal ambitions are turned upside down, your perspective changes, and you observe happenings in a new light. You are awakened to much more around you because you are not so preoccupied with yourself.

Writing is exhausting when we want to churn out superior new ideas constantly. We are tempted to settle for mediocre fill-ins. "Of making many books there is no end, and much study is a weariness of the flesh." Where does fresh vision and dynamism come from? "If any of you lacks wisdom, let him ask God, who gives to all men generously" for "(you) have clothed yourselves with the new spiritual self, which is ever in the process of being renewed and remolded into fuller and more perfect knowledge upon knowledge."[6]

People who love work. Writing is like having a baby. First comes the moment of ecstasy in which you conceive the idea. Then come hours and maybe months of sweaty struggle as the idea slowly develops, months when the still-unformed, increasingly cumbersome idea restricts your schedule and burdens you. Bringing the writing to birth is a thoroughly down-to-earth business.

Real writers discipline themselves to write a certain number of hours or to produce a certain number of words each day. "No professional writer can afford to write when he feels like it. If he waits until he is in the mood, till he has the inspiration, as he says, he waits indefinitely and ends by producing little or nothing. The professional writer creates the mood. He has his inspiration, too, but he controls and subdues it to his bidding."[7] Almost every writer procrastinates. So we must stubbornly maintain regular writing habits. Set aside a definite time for writing each day or each week. Use the part of the day when you can think most clearly. Ruthlessly screen out distractions— avoid visitors and leave your mail unopened during this period. To find a quiet time you may have to work in the middle of the night: many great writers have done so. Learn to use periods of inactivity or manual work—when you are riding a bus or waiting for someone or washing dishes or ironing—to mentally play with the ideas you are writing about. Then you will come to your desk ready to write.

You must be systematic in your work hours, in your research procedures, and in the organization of your piece. You must be meticulous about details—checking facts for accuracy, producing clean manuscripts, and meeting deadlines. You must be willing to rewrite a piece several times.

If you are going to glorify God as an artist, you owe it to God to master the art as well as any non-Christian. Beginning as a craftsman, you can grow to be an artist. If you are not a fulltime writer, your job can be a crucible of experience in which you discover stories, deepen your insight, and experience the reality of God in everyday circumstances.

As a writer you must be both realistic and idealistic— meeting deadlines and dreaming dreams. You will want to combine the broadest possible background with a firm dedication to duty.

People who love to communicate. Some who love words and ideas and system do not ache to communicate. But you need such enthusiasm if you are to over-come the problems of a writer and keep on producing manuscripts.

What are these problems? Lack of adequate pay, lack of training, lack of time, and lack of a quiet place to work. Many of us would rather teach and evangelize people face to face than reach them through writing done in isolation. Revising a manuscript is frustrating, and preparing clean copies for a publisher is boring and tiring. You may not be skilled in the language in which you want to write. Working with ideas and words can draw you away from involvement with people so that you become theoretical and callous.

Do these problems discourage you? God has often used discouraged and hesitant men. When He called Moses, the prophet answered, "Who am I that I should go to Pharaoh and bring the sons of Israel out of Egypt? . . . They will not believe me or listen to my voice. . . Oh my Lord, I am not eloquent, either heretofore or since thou hast spoken to thy servant. But I am slow of speech and of tongue. . . Oh my Lord, send, I pray, some other person."

Jeremiah said, "Ah Lord God, I do not know how to speak, for I am only a youth." Gideon asked, "Pray, Lord, how can I deliver Israel? My clan is the weakest in Manasseh and I am the least in my family." Isaiah confessed, "I am lost—for I am a man of unclean lips." Amos said plainly, "I am no prophet, nor a prophet's son. But I am a herdsman, and a dresser of sycamore trees."

But Amos went on to say how he became the Lord's spokeman. "And the Lord took me as I followed the flock, and the Lord said to me, 'Go, prophesy to my people.'"[8]

Whom has God called to speak to your people? Could this be an activity through which you could show your love to God, share with your fellowmen, help your nation in its growing years, and express your own creativity? Pray about your priorities see where Christian writing fits in.

---

[1] Isaiah 40:12-13

[2] Song of Solomon 2 :10-13.

[3] Arthur Miller.

[4] Dick Dowsen, "'The Challenge of the Laity, " *The Messago, Man, and Missions*. Manila: Philippine Inter-Varsity Christian Fellowship, 1971, p. 48

[5] Herbert Butterfield. *Christianity and History* London: Fontana Hooks.1980, p 16.

[6] Verses in the paragraph are: Ecclesiastes 12:12; James1:5; and Colossians 3:10. Amplified.

[7] W. Somerset Maugham, *The Summing Up*, New York: Doubleday and Co., Inc., p 181.

[8] Verses in this section are: Exodus 3:11-4:13: Jeremiah 1:6; Isaiah 6:5; Amos 7:14-15

3.   WHO WILL READ?

Who reads Christian writing? Sophisticated students, who are also reading Camus and Nietzsche. Radical students who are also reading Marx and Lenin. Tenant farmers with dried buffalo dung under their finger nails. Wealthy matrons. Market vendors. Barely literate young mothers. Curious children. Grandfathers sitting in tea shops.

Because they are different, these people need different kinds of writing. So, before you write, you must choose your audience.

The apostles knew their audiences, and varied their communication accordingly. For Jews, their framework was the law of Moses and the prophets. They gave Christ's credentials in terms of the scriptures. Paul declared "nothing but what the prophets and Moses said would come to pass." Christ himself, "beginning with Moses and all the prophets interpreted to them in all the scriptures the things concerning himself." Their common gospel was that "Christ died for our sins according to the scriptures. . . " and their sermons pulsate with scriptural quotes.[1]

But when they preached to pagans, they dropped the emphasis on the law and the prophets. What did the pagans care about Jewish history? Instead, the apostles spoke of how God may be discovered through nature and conscience, how God has provided for man's temporal needs, how God is now providing for man's spiritual needs, and how the pagans should turn from the frail power of their idols to the great power of God.

So when Paul preached in a Jewish synagogue in Antioch of Pisidia, he spoke of Jesus, the scriptural Messiah. Then he showed how Christ's resurrection had brought mankind far beyond the law of Moses. Some listeners were fascinated. Others were furious—not because they misunderstood, but because they understood only too well.

But in pagan Lystra it was different. Here Paul performed a miraculous cure, leading the people to believe that he was a god. With this misunderstanding, Paul could not preach on Christ's death and resurrection. The people did not even have any notion of one God. So Paul preached on theism. He spoke of "the living God who made the heaven and the earth and the sea and all that is in them"— the God who "gave you rains and fruitful seasons, satisfying your hearts with food and gladness." He could not ex plain what God would do for them until they understood who God was.

Later Paul went to Athens. Whereas the Lystrans were simple, the Athenians were sophisticated pagans. They invited Paul to present his teaching in their most venerable court, so that they could decide whether his ideas contributed to the public welfare. Here Paul began with the Athenians' ideas about God and led them to a vision of the great God. He quoted the Greek poets when he made the point that we are all the offspring of God. Therefore, he said, we should not expect God either to be distant or to be captured in idols. Rather we should look for a way to relate to God personally. And now this way has been provided in Jesus Christ, who has demonstrated his own uniqueness by rising from the dead.

No man knew better than Paul when to present his Hebrew, Greek, or Roman credentials. While keeping the same content, he willingly changed the form of his communication according to his audience. He realized that the gospel is something that God has done, not a series of words describing what happened. So he was willing to start where his listeners were. We must do this too.

How do you write for one audience? First, you must decide what the various audiences are. Where are the divisions among your people? You see racial, ethnic, and language differences. Social classes. Regional contrasts. Educational, economic, political, and religious variations. Women and men have different lifestyles. Many young people live in a more secular, materialistic world than the old traditionalists. Amid all these contrasts, what are the **significant** divisions? What are the major groupings of your people?

Once you have picked out an audience, the following questions can help you analyze them.

What needs or problems do they feel? All men have some area in which they are dissatisfied, longing, and seeking. All men's hearts are restless for the true resting place. There is a spiritual vacuum even in the heart of the traditional farmer—and the modern Communist. So if you write about their real worries, people will read.

But make certain you write about needs that your audience **does** feel—not about needs you **think that they should** feel. Otherwise you will be "scratching where it does not itch." Do not be like a relief agency which sent thousands of cans of cheese to the Montagnards of Vietnam. The Montagnards abhorred cheese. But they liked the gift because, after they had dumped out the cheese, they found the cans very useful! How tragic if our publications are so irrelevant that they are only used for wrapping meat in the market.

Many Asians fear evil spirits. So if we are relating to their needs, maybe we should present Christ's death not so much as a substitution for their guilt but rather as a victory over the powers of darkness.

Some Asians worry that they will not be an academic success and will shame their family. Others have sex conflicts. Some are overwhelmed by poverty, while still others pour themselves into efforts for a social revolution. Your audience may cry out for friendship, a sense of identity, a purpose, hope, removal of guilt, a sense of racial or national significance, meaning in work, freedom from parents, or even the ability to love. What are their felt needs?

What are their values and aspirations? What do they feel will bring them the good life? Some trust in material success. Others believe a change in the structure of government would solve their problems. Others put their faith in romantic love. Or your audience may live for academic or professional success, family pride, pleasure, friendship, community solidarity, or simply for the joy of a flourishing family.

An audience's needs and values are a writer's **points of contact.** We write in terms of the fluidity of life if our audience is Buddhist. We speak of imperialism, the bourgeoisie, and the people's struggle if they are Marxist. We take off from issues covered in the press if they are newspaper-readers. We use popular songs as our reference point if their heads are full of these tunes and lyrics. We begin with the known and progress to the unknown.

What communication styles do they respect and respond to? Do they like frankness or subtlety? Formality or informality? Poetry and myth, or histories, or concrete proverbs? Abstract ideas, or references to tangible things?

What kinds of publications do they normally read? Some lose themselves in popular fiction and comics. They want light, lively reading matter. Others, who read for information but not entertainment, want solid content— " people who will read—holding small print up to their eyes under 25-watt bulbs while rediffusion sets blare, children yell, societies dance, and drunks fight, all within yards of them—will read anything provided it is not frivolous, is related to something significant for them, and that they can make intellectual contact with it."[2] What kind of publication does your chosen audience read normally?

Do they make decisions as groups or as individuals? Many Asians act in groups. Kin, neighbors, and friends like to take new steps together. We should cooperate with these ties. We should not break people apart but rather should bind them together and bring them to the Lord Jesus Christ as a group. We should not primarily encourage the conversion of lone oddballs and rebels and those who are already alienated from their families. Instead, we should write materials that will lead whole groups into the family of Christ.

Research has demonstrated that when a person is faced with a decision, he usually will not make it just on the basis of information that comes to him through the mass media. He will also look to other people whom he respects. Voters look to other voters when they vote, rather than relying on what they hear over the radio or read in the newspaper. Doctors look to their colleagues when they prescribe new drugs. When women go marketing, they ask mothers of large families for advice on the best buys. And when women choose fashions, they look to young women to set the pace.

Sometimes these "opinion leaders" will be fathers. At other times they will be mothers. In some places old men will lead, while in other localities young professionals will exert the most influence. In any case, the ideas presented by mass media may be reinforced or rejected by such "opinion leaders," so it is important to write especially for them. None of our readers lives in a social vacuum.

What are their ideas of God? First the Christian writer looks for **points of contact** in his audience's needs and values. Then he looks for **points of confrontation** between his faith and theirs. It is important to place conflicting beliefs in unmistakable contrast. Otherwise a Christian teaching may simply be added to a traditional belief, rather than substituted for it.

Your audience's idea of God may be one point of confrontation. A secular audience may believe that only the uneducated still believe in God. Some fear that God is too far away to help us much. Others believe they can build up merit to bargain with God.

What are their ideas of the supernatural? Many who doubt God's existence still believe in the supernatural— ghosts, spirits, and the power of witchcraft and sorcery. Even sophisticated young people will usually avoid "haunted" places at night. Some who give lip service to Islam or Christianity are really much more aware of the spirits than they are of Allah or God. This can be a point of both contact and confrontation.

What are their ideas of Christ? Do they see Him as a great teacher? A prophet inferior to Mohammed? A dead Savior? A mystical deity? Or the Creator, Sustainer, and Savior of the world, who rose from the dead in history and is living now?

What are their ideas of man? Why do we exist? How can we find fulfillment? Are we the result of a mindless evolutionary process?

Is our purpose to live honorably and maintain the family heritage? Or do we have to find our own purpose in our work, our pleasures, our love, and our contributions to the world? Is man progressing or falling apart? Can man achieve salvation through his own good works? Your audience's view of man may be contrasted with the Christian teaching that man is made beautifully in the image of God, made to need communion with God, but guilty of rupturing that communion, and in need of God's grace for its restoration.

What could be your initial points of contact in communicating to this audience? Now you are ready to apply your knowledge of your audience. Let us suppose, for example, that your audience is Muslim. Like you, they believe in one holy and loving God, the Creator and Sustainer of the world, who has revealed himself in his holy Word. Man's purpose is to know and live in obedience to God. But there is no redemption. God sends his truth, but never comes. Man relates to God either through his own good works or through God's arbitrary forgiveness. Sin is not such a central doctrine.

What points of contact can you find? Here are some ideas.

Begin with their understanding of the nature of God, and enrich it. In today's atheistic world, Muslims appreciate defenses of theism. Write about God's standard of holiness, which they value. Then move to a point of confrontation by showing that they are unworthy to stand in the presence of such a holy God.

Begin with their concept of sin as defilement and then demonstrate by reference to specific sins like hatred and feuds, that they can never measure up to their ideal.

Begin with God in this holiness and love. Show how He has revealed himself in creation and then in Old Testament history. Use Old Testament stories which are also in the Koran. Then show how the law was not enough, so God revealed himself at last in Christ.

Teach the meaning of Christ, the suffering Servant, as Muslims also hear about Jesus, the servant of God.

Since Muslims are human, relate to their human needs—poverty, loss of a loved one, insecurity about the future. Many modern Muslims no longer believe their own religion's stories about, for example, Adam and Eve. Then relate to them as to materialists.

Write stories about people who are experiencing and demonstrating a holiness and love so radical that it convicts and challenges the reader. Make these stories exciting, appealing, believable, and in the traditional story style. Especially use stories of converted Muslims.

Serialize the story of a Muslim village conversion, either true or fictional. This helps the reader see Christianity as a more real possibility for him.

Write chants like their traditional chants.

Since many Muslims still fear spirits, they need what pagans need—victory over the powers of darkness. Write about how Christ brings this.

Start out with an appreciation for some aspect of their Muslim heritage, such as the equality of all races, or the ideal of social solidarity.

At what points should you contrast your message with their beliefs? Now you apply your knowledge as you find points of confrontation. To Muslims you may say, "Your God is too far. It is possible to know God personally in everyday human life." You may contrast the God who only reveals himself with the God who comes in the flesh. You may contrast the Muslim view that man is largely a fated robot with the Christian view that man has free will. You may contrast their dependence on good works with the Christian dependence on the grace of God. You may contrast their view that Christ was snatched off the cross and saved from death with the evidence for the real death and resurrection of Christ in history. You may contrast their experience of feeling lost with the Christian experience of feeling found. You may contrast their memorized prayers with their need for deeply personal communication with God in their own tongue. You may do word studies on the Christian and Muslim meanings of "grace" or "revelation" or "crucifixion ."

Finally, when choosing your audience, do not forget to write for the people of God. All the biblical authors wrote to the people of God. The New Testament says we are given gifts, like writing, so that we can help each other grow up to maturity. So look at the believers in your country. What are their needs? Is there a generation gap? Division over personalities? Concentration on externals? Fear of non-Christians? Ignorance of the Bible? Laziness and poor use of time? Materialism? Write to these needs.

When teaching believers something, new, you should directly confront their previous beliefs. If you are teaching students the doctrine of the Church, put their subconscious reservations into words at the beginning:

"Well . . . .we study the Bible in our student fellowship. We listen to leaders expound the Word. We evangelize on campus, and we have real fellowship together. That's enough, isn't it? Why bother with a church?" Or if you are emphasizing the importance of doctrine: "Doctrine? Ugh! Leave that to theologians. I just believe in Jesus. I know He's changed my life. That's enough for me!" Or if you are writing on pornography: "No sex before marriage. No homosexual playing around. All right. But I'm human. I have sex drives. Don't these magazines have a cathartic effect? They give a sort of vicarious enjoyment and provide an outlet for it all. And it doesn't do anyone any harm." If you clearly contrast your audience's beliefs with your teaching, your impact will be much stronger.

It is not enough to write the truth. You must write to the concerns of a specific audience. "The fisherman must think like the fish if he expects to catch any of them." We are not just reaching souls, but communicating to "sensitive, thinking, feeling persons, complex persons, over whose minds have poured whole centuries of history and habit, custom and culture. " We must begin wherever they are.

---

1   Verses in this paragraph are: Acts 26:22; Luke 24:27; and 1Cor 15:3.

2   Andrew Walls quoted in Joyce Chaplin's *Adventure with a Pen* Kumasi, Ghana: African Christian Press, 1966, p. 15.

4.   WHAT TO WRITE

Christian writing is not necessarily writing about religious subject matter, but it is writing from the **perspective** of a Christian philosophy of life.

Knowing God affects our view of all physical, social, psychological, intellectual, and spiritual experience. We may write about money, sports, sex, sickness, or politics. In all these practical spheres God is relevant.

Intellectual disciplines are also part of his domain. When we study natural science, we are thinking God's thoughts after Him. When we study the arts, we are appreciating what men have done when acting in the image of God, the great Creator. When working for social justice, we sweat for ideals stemming from God's law.

Christian writers must deal with the whole diverse scope of life, because Christ is Lord of all.

How do we go about covering a topic from a Christian perspective? Too many Christian writers learn how to present a subject without learning how to think it through. So they write well and say nothing. Or they write well and express non-Christian philosophies. Or they present only half of the truth.

As a writer, you cannot be merely a skillful technician who can put an idea into words when someone hands you the idea. You must be a man who experiences life—the rise in prices, the suspension of civil liberties, a split in you church, the death of your mother—who understands these experiences from a Christian point of view, and who can creatively analyze them in such a way that you give light and direction to others. No matter how skillfully you may use words, it is only when you can cover a subject adequately that you are really a writer. Learning to write means learning to think, too.

Suppose your society is reverberating with demonstrations and political upheaval. So you want to formulate a Christian view of society. What will you say?

First, consider the possible views. (1) Our society is good enough as it is, with mild reforms. (2) Our society is in bad shape, and needs radical reform. (3) Our social structure is impossible, and demands violent revolution. (4) Our society is in bad shape, and needs mass conversion to Christ. (5) Christians should not get deeply involved in society.

How will you choose among these views? Will you appeal to your own reason? To the teaching of your Christian fellowship? To the general majority view? All of these may be warped by human ignorance and selfishness. You need a guide independent of your culture and your reason. Fortunately, God has given us such a guide in His Word. So the Bible must be your constant reference when you are covering a topic from a Christian perspective.

But how do you find biblical truth on a particular topic? One Bible passage may turn out to be only a small part of God's revelation on the subject. For example, Christ said we should not pile up treasure on earth. But the apostle Paul said that a Christian who does not provide for the financial needs of his household is worse than an infidel. If you base your writing on only one of these passages, your piece will be lopsided and will not represent God's full truth.

So you need to search the "whole counsel of God," the Old Testament and the New, the Epistles and the Gospels, the stories and the doctrinal sections. Then build general principles from the sum of the specific teachings on the topic you are studying.

"That's hopeless! I would never have time for that!" you may sigh in despair. But someone in your country must make time for it. Along with pastors and teachers, we writers are responsible for guiding God's people in our own nations. If you lead your people astray because of careless research, will you dare to whine, "I had no time to really study the Bible?" You cannot depend forever on foreign books. Who is ready to interpret and apply God's truth to daily life in your country?

To find biblical passages which pertain to your topic, use concordances, commentaries, Bible dictionaries, and relevant books. Borrow these from pastors, Christian friends, or the library of a theological seminary.

Divide your topic into several sub-topics, and investigate these. When researching a biblical view of society, for example, you can investigate what the Bible has to say about social classes, distribution of wealth, social change, violence, judgment of society, prosperity of society, the nature of man, the purpose of society, the basis of law, citizenship, government, nationalism, imperialism, God's interaction with society throughout history, Christian interaction with society, et cetera.

When you find a relevant passage, observe it, interpret it, and apply it. Ask: What does it say? What did it mean to those to whom it was written ? What does it mean for us today?

In a narrative passage, focus on the central action. Find out who was involved, how, where, when, why, and with what results. In an explanatory section, discover who was writing, and why: who the readers were, and what their context was; what is the central thought of each paragraph; how the paragraphs are related; and what is the major teaching of the passage as a whole.

What does this teach about God, Christ, the Holy Spirit, man, and life in general? How can I respond? Is there a good or bad example? A command? A promise? These questions will help you apply the truth.

Some passages are very difficult. In general, symbolic passages must be interpreted in light of plain teaching passages found elsewhere. Perplexing incidental verses must be viewed in light of the systematic teaching contained in doctrinal books like Romans or Galatians. The New Testament interprets the Old Testament, and the Epistles interpret the Gospels.

Gradually you should form principles for your own Christian world view. Then, when you react to a contemporary issue, you can be guided by the basic truths you have stored up.

For example, a Christian world view emphasizes the existence of the supernatural. Often we think like atheists, as if the material world were what really counted. But a Christian world view reminds us that this is not a world owned and controlled by men, but a world formed by God, maintained by God, worried over by God, and died for by God. There are forces and powers in the world beyond those we can perceive and measure. Life continues beyond history. This is not a closed natural universe.

Man is both honorable and evil in a Christian world view. Man is higher than the angels, next to God, worth more than all the things in the world put together. God has honored man by making man in his own image. Men are personalities, not machines or animals. Men are models of God, not just sinners. God has also honored many by loving him and expecting him to be able to love in return. God has honored man by becoming a man. God has honored man by dying for man. So we value every man, and cannot view any man as merely the sum of his functions.

But all men, the criminals and the respectable alike, are also sinners, willfully loving themselves more than God. Even society's good men are condemned by their self-righteousness. Knowing human nature, then we habitually expect moral conflict. We are ready for evil, not surprised by it. We can never sell out to the establishment, but instead must continually judge—including ourselves in the judgment.

A Christian world view demands a total fanatic dedication to Christ. "The Bible itself says very little commending moderation. Does the Bible suggest anywhere that we are to be moderately good, moderately holy, moderately zealous? Or does it anywhere permit us to be just moderately selfish and moderately self-indulgent? The history of the Old Testament might be described as the history of a people who wanted to be moderate and tolerant in their religion, and how God would not permit this."[1]

What is the basis of truth for you? What is your attitude to beauty in the world? To the meaning of Christ's cross? To the bond that unites all Christians? To the coming return of our Lord? These should become central strands in your world view. If you want to be a writer rather than a propagandist, you must read, think, and ask questions. There is no short cut. You must go alone to encounter the vision that God will give you.

Yevgeny Yevtushenko has a vision of Communism as the social system that liberates all men. Alexander Solzhenitsyn has a vision of the beauty and indestructibility of the individual. Chaim Potok has a vision of how men find meaning in life through friendship, loving, suffering, faith in God, and confidence in a historic tradition. Writers from Franz Kafka to John Updike have had a vision of man lost in the universe. These are the messages of great writers today. What is your vision?

When choosing a topic, ask yourself these questions:

What is inside me? What do I have to say? What unique experiences have I had? Write what you know. "A writer who does not speak out of a full experience will use wooden words, lifeless words, which have a paralysis in their tails," said Henry Thoreau .

What are people reading and talking about? What are the hottest topics? To avoid controversial issues is irresponsible, because these are exactly the issues on which people need guidance. Christians must never refuse to look at anything in life: what we cannot see we cannot grapple with. We must "see life steadily and see it whole."

Can I find enough information on the subject? No one wants your opinions unless you are famous. But many will publish your facts if they are accurate, interesting, and significant. Get data from observations, interviews, surveys, reading, organization records, public records, public information bureaus, conferences, and personal experience. For each source, ask: Is this reliable? Up to date? Balanced? Where can I find out the other side?

Can I find a publisher for this?

Can I make this interesting? Does it have dramatic potential? Human interest? Unusual details?

What do the people of God need? In choosing a topic, do not overlook Bible stories. Many Christians in your country have never read the Old Testament. They need truth from God's Word more than they need your opinions on Christian living—and they need not only snippings from the Gospels and the Psalms, but the whole teaching from Genesis to the Song of Solomon to Habakkuk to Jude.

Let us put the biblical narrative into contemporary dramas and stories, and take it to the people. Bible stories make sense in Asia, because the biblical cultures were much like Asian folk cultures are today. Already thousands of Hindus have discovered the message of the Old and New Testaments through dramas.

Here is a list of topics to stimulate your imagination. Some are aimed to teach Christians, others to evangelize. Still others are for the whole community. This list is merely a starting point for you.

1. **Money**
> How to budget
> How to keep out of debt
> God and your money

2. **Sex and love**
> Why did God create sex?
> What can I do with my sexual desires?
> Aren't sexy movies and books educational?
> How can I get to know "prospects" well?
> What is the place of parents and chaperones during courtship?
> How do you know when you have met "the one"?
> Where love comes from?
> Keeping romance in marriage
> Practical considerations for marriage

3. **Family**
> How to communicate with your parents, children, husband, wife.
> How to relate to non-Christian parents.
> How to manage a Christian home.
> What children need, how to raise children.

What teenagers need.
Why we have juvenile delinquency.
The fragmenting urban family, problems of urban living
Family planning.
Women's liberation.

4. Prominent People

5. Health
Causes of illness: spirits?
Nutrition, God's concern for our bodies.
Various common illnesses and what to do for them.
Depression.
Tension.
Sin and sickness.
Stories of handicapped people who live success.

6. Education
How to study, how to motivate yourself.
How to set priorities and budget your time.
What is truth? What is its basis?
Articles and books relating a Christian world view to psychology, education, business administration, biology, history, geography, economics, agriculture, community development, et cetera.

7. National characteristics, national history
The national Church in national history.
Some national value, its good and bad sides in light of God's law.
Should a Christian be a nationalist?

8. Loneliness and friendship
How and when to be a friend.
How to break out of your "shell" and meet people.
When you have quarrelled . . . . .
When you are worried . . . . .
If you are new in the city . . . . .
If you have a new job . . . . .

9. Tragedy
What is death?
What happens when someone dies?
Why does God allow pain and sickness?
Why does God allow typhoons?
What can we do about them?
Why does God allow an unjust society?
What can we do about it?

Stories of how local Christians have helped in typhoons, floods, or epidemics.
Stories of what Christians have done in social reform.
Miraculous rescues from tragedy in answer to prayer.
What Christians have learned through pain and suffering.

10. The full, pleasurable life

What to do if life is boring God wants you to have a full, dynamic life.
Stewardship, priorities in the use of time and money.
What is worldliness?
A fashionable witness.
Brain drain.
How is city Christianity different from rural Christianity?
Horoscopes and astrology.
Guidelines for a Christian in business.

11. People of God

Stories of individual Christians in various sections of your cities—slums, high rise apartments, rustic neighborhoods, wealthy sections, sailors on ships.
Stories of individual Christians from various rural regions.
Stories of individual Christians in other countries.
Stories of individual Christians throughout history.
Stories of groups of Christians in all the above categories.

12. What the Bible says

Bible story in contemporary form.
Exposition of a single passage.
Topical study of some subject in Scripture.

13. What Christians believe—and why

Who made who? Is God a creation of man's imagination, or is man a creation of God's?
Who is God? How do we know He exists? What difference does it make?
Is it only the uneducated who believe in the super-natural?
Who is Christ? What difference does He make?
Was Christ a Westerner?
Why did Christ die?
Does it matter whether Christ rose from the dead?
What is man really like? What is human life all about? What are we heading for? Will we be happy when we get there?
"Lost," "sinful"—what do these mean?
Can you change man when you change the social structure?
Is guilt just psychological?
What is the Church good for?

Spirits and the Holy Spirit.
Where is history going? Jesus is coming again
How can a man live with God day by day?
God's freedom and discipline.
What happens when a Christian sins.
How do we know the Bible is reliable?
Are miracles possible?

14. Practical Christian living

How to pray
How to understand the Bible
How to meet God everyday
How to tell your friends about God
How to find out God's will
How to to have a group Bible study
How to help a new Christian
How to have a Christian festival
How to deal with anger and resentment
How to develop a cleaner mind
Gossip
What to do when you have a personality clash
Is there a generation gap in your church?
Creative tension in the Church
How to speak, write or lead discussions
Guidelines for leaders
How to teach
How to do personal counselling
Baptism
What should laymen do?
How to be a creative Christian in the military service
How to be a creative Christian nurse
How to be a creative Christian in the mass media
How to be a creative Christian farmer

15. Christian faith and other faiths

Marx and Christ
The way to God: drugs?
Making merit
What are you making money for? Just a TV and a stereo?
Is human love enough?
Are Christian conversions just psychological?
Can a scientist believe Christ is God?
Can you believe in the supernatural without believing in
        superstition?
Can an artist keep his integrity and hold Christian dogma ?
Existentialism
Determinism
Christ and Buddhism

Christ and Islam
Christ and the Spirits
Why can't you adhere to your old religion while believing in
    Christ?
"Religion is the opiate of the people."
"I can get along without God."
"It doesn't matter what you believe, as long as you are
    sincere."

16-19. Fiction, parables, poetry, and comics.

---

1   Michael Griftiths, *Take My Life* Chicago: Inter-Varsity Press, 1967,
     p 12.

5.   HOW TO WRITE

Writing an Article

Why do we write? To communicate to our reader. To provoke him, to move him. Often to change him, either by deepening his life or by transforming it.

Human communication is not an academic exercise. So when we write articles we must throw away our formal term paper writing style. You may respect lofty, abstract, metaphorical, and highly conceptualized literature. But that does not arrest the attention of the common man who wants practical information. It does not hold the executive the fast-moving world. For them you must write with directness, human interest, action and brevity. You must describe things as they are. You must use concrete terms. You must write clearly and dramatically.

Look at advertisements. Their messages are striking and unmistakable because they are **simple.** We dare not blunt the impact of our good news by covering it over with jargon, with euphemisms, with the padding of big words, or with impersonal, intellectual language.

"Seeing that we have such hope, we use great plain ness of speech" (ll Cor. 3:12). We employ common words. We demonstrate the power and beauty of simple sentences. We keep our paragraphs short.

We also **limit the focus.** When writing how Christ is a solution to problems, don't list every problem a person might have. Instead, explore one or two problems in depth. Writing which is narrow and deep—which sticks to one idea and investigates all its angles—has "class." Likewise, choose a manageable topic.

You can **bring your writing to life** if you will follow these suggestions:

Use **action illustrations** to make your writing dramatic. Show rather than tell. Use stories for your examples.

Use people in your illustrations. Nothing interests people more than people. Make your characters human by giving details about their physical appearances and emotional temperaments. Fictional characters are perfectly acceptable.

Use **dialogue** between your characters.

Use **concrete, specific words to describe** sights, noises, smells, heat, wetness and emotional feelings like fear, relaxation, boredom, or tiredness.

Use **questions or statements to the reader.** "What does it mean to be a Christian and a nationalist?"

Use **strong verbs.**

Use references to current issues, fashions, songs, games and pastimes, ideas, and news events.

Use references to **local and national surroundings and feelings**—typhoons, rice harvests, tenants in debt, homeless migrants to the city, feasts, local values, local foods, local industrial products.

Use **local and national phrases, colloquial expressions, and proverbs.**

Use **fresh and unusual details.**

Since we want to affect our reader's decisions and behavior, we need to penetrate beyond his mind to the seat of his will. We must stir him, not by telling him facts but by showing him human situations with which he can identify.

How to Gather Information

Choose a topic that will provoke a response. Get clear in your mind what the problem is. State the problem concisely. Decide who this is a problem for–who your readers are.

Start keeping a file for this article. Have a "jotting sheet" in the file, on which you can jot down relevant ideas and illustrations from time to time. Gradually, as some sub-topics emerge out of your jottings, you'll want to try to make a tentative outline for your article.

Pray about this article ofen. Ask God to teach you truth in relation to it, and to use it to glorify Him and to genuinely help other people. Keep your motives and priorities right.

Try to find biblical principles and biblical illustrations of this subject to guide your own thinking. Mentally review what you have read in the Bible so far: has this subject been touched? You may want to use a topical concordance of the Bible to help you find references. Or you may ask other Christians to suggest some passages where this topic is considered. Take brief notes on these principles and illustrations, and record the references.

Think through your own experiences on this subject. Write these down quickly, without attempt to polish . Don't worry about your style at this stage: you are just pinning down information.

Ask other Christians to suggest books or articles on this subject. Browse through Christian libraries, including the libraries of your friends. Read the best materials you find, and take notes.

Think of experiences of other people you know. Write these down. The more illustrations you compile at this stage, the better.

When you are in casual conversation with others who might have some ideas on this topic, bring it up. Explain that you are doing some research on it. Afterwards jot down the best ideas that were shared.

Think about this topic during "blank time" . . . . riding the bus, waiting for your friends, doing manual jobs. Look for illustrations in daily life.

How to Put Your Information into Your Article

Decide what your sub-topics will be. Sort out your data so that each piece of information falls under some sub-topic You may want to cut up your notes so that you can gather the ideas for each sub-topic into a separate pile. For this reason, never take notes on both sides of a page.

Choose the best illustrations. Put the rest aside.

Decide the order of your sub-topics. Plan to grab your reader's attention with your first words. You must hit him with the significance of your article, and must establish your authonrity. You must attack the subject from where the reader looks at it, and must indicate how the topic affects him. Some editors consider the first paragraphs the most important.

How do you start? You can:

        describe a setting
        tell a brief, active story to illustrate your topic
        directly address the reader with a statement or

        question
state a problem
flash out a striking thought
summarize your theme

In the body of your article you may have several points, each with qualifications, examples, applications, or other sub-points. Organize so that everything relating to one point appears together, not straggling throughout the whole article. Each sentence should lead into the next, and each paragraph should be distinct yet relate to the one that follows. Your beginning, end, and middle should point to the same theme. Balance and brighten your explanations by occasional illustrations.

How do you end? You can write a:

(a) summary.
(b) "snapper." This is a surprise ending, which leaves the reader laughing, gasping, crying, or pondering.
(c) practical application. What is the reader supposed to do about it all?

Write the first sentence after you have planned the structure. By now you have done enough research that your question is not "What shall I say?" but "Which shall I say first?"

You will need to rewrite when you finish. Inspirations bubbled up while you wrote. You added extra information. Perhaps you rearranged the order you have planned. Now check the logic. Is it still a clear progression of ideas? Is it still a unified whole?

Scratch out all unnecessary words and random repetitions. Replace vague words with concrete ones, impersonal words with colorful ones. Change passive constructions to active. Add questions to make boring sections more lively. Then smooth out the transitions so that the article will flow as if it had just now tumbled out of your thoughts!

Some writers work best on a team. A team can:

- choose a topic
- brainstorm on its controversial aspects
- assign each member to
- research certain aspects if necessary
- construct an outline or plot line
- assign each member to write one part
- exchange and critique each others' chapters

• pray for each other

Each step must have a deadline. If team meetings are to be more than a pooling of ignorance, someone must be well-organized. Periodically he must remind others of their main topics and deadlines. They in turn must honor him, so that he will not grow discouraged and fall silent.

WRITING A STORY

Everybody loves to hear stories. Well-written stories are always interesting because they are made up of fast moving dialogue, concrete details, action, people, and simplicity. Readers identify more readily with story situations than they do with facts in an intellectual article.

Plot

"A short story occurs in the middle of life. A door opens on a scene where people are talking, acting, and reflecting. They are caught in a few moments of intensity and then the door must close—the story is finished."

A story revolves around a **problem,** its crisis, and its resolution. In the opening paragraphs you introduce the problem, the setting, the characters, and the emotional tone. You do not state these bluntly, but subtly and gradually reveal them through action as the story moves along.

The problem involves **two opposing forces:** man versus a typhoon, Christian convictions versus a temptation to bribe a public official. The keener the conflict, the sharper the suspense.

As the story progresses, the problem gets worse. Complications arise, new threats press in, the tension crescendos. The characters reach a crisis. Here the action hangs in suspension momentarily—while the reader gobbles up the page to find out what will happen.

The climax is reached: the conflict is settled, either by the character's decision or by some combination of external forces. These forces cannot appear suddenly at this point; they must have been somewhere in the story from the beginning if the climax is to appear natural.

The **resolution,** which ties up loose ends and finishes the story, should follow right away so that the tingling taste of the climax is not diluted. You do not have to draw a moral or even reach a formal conclusion: simply show the state of your characters after the crisis—relaxing, despairing, or starting something new.

Action and suspense should be maximized. "The leaves fluttered" suggests a wind blowing. "The tin can glittered in the ditch, and the mango tree cast a black shadow" shows that it is a moonlight night. You must carefully select details that will either increase the dramatic tension of your plot, make your characters more alive or authenticate your setting: throw out other details.

A few symbols may deepen your story. A storm, for example, may symbolize the powerful forces which threaten your character. The daily roving vendor may symbolize the regular passage of time. A child singing at his play may symbolize innocence. A small fire at the beginning of the story may symbolize a large conflagration at the end.

You may want to write a modern "plotless" short story—merely a succession of moments in the lives of certain characters, without climax or major struggle. This style has developed because twentieth century writers see man increasingly controlled by bureaucracies and machines, lacking individual moral fiber and too unsure of moral absolutes to make decisive choices. Such men only question; they rarely triumph. They experience life in fragments, without passing any judgments. They are not worth much, by their own standards everything is relative, and so is their own value.

With cholera, famines, corrupt governments, unequal distribution of wealth, hypocritical friends, and personal failures, we Christians know well enough that there is paradox and ambiguity in life. But we are confident that the law and plan of God still structure nature and history somewhere behind the contradictions. Man is worth everything, being created in the image of God and being the object of God's redemptive sacrifice. So we do not worship relativity.

Certainly you can write a "plotless" short story as a Christian. Whichever style you choose, avoid naive optimism, unrealistic clarity in your character's motives, absolute victories, or grand characters. Today's heroes are thoroughly fallible and human.

Characters

Make each character a distinct personality. How does he walk? Does he laugh often? Is he pensive, or excitable, or friendly to strangers? How tall is he? How much does he weigh? Does he wear glasses, or slouch, or gesture with hands?

You may reveal your character's personality by his physical traits; by quick glimpses into the childhood experiences which have molded his unconscious values; by the way he relates to other people; by the way he relates to God; by his political outlook, his job and its economic status, his race, his social position, his neighborhood, and his family.

Your character's speech will also indicate his intelligence, his education, his interests, and his temperament. Each character should speak with a slightly different rhythm, vocabulary, and length of sentence.

Dialogue is more a revelation of characters and a vehicle for action than it is a wooden exchange of information. To be realistic your dialogue should include interruptions and some broken sentences when a character is searching for words.

Naturally you cannot describe your characters fully: you must select a few traits to represent the whole. The more particular, the better. A certain movement of the elbows, a hesitation in speaking, a general sullennes, and habitually unpolished shoes—these may be the traits selcted to stand for one character.

You will want to explore the mental processes which make your characters behave as they do. But do not let the whole action be mental.

Theme

If your story is not based on a profound moral view, its end will be banal. Life is not just squabbles and fears, and acquisitions and achievements, and prayers and religious services, and feasts and marketing. There are bigger things. Love. The holiness of God and the way He has expressed this loveliness in the beauty of earth. The power of evil Man in the image of God, man in his evil, man afraid of the twentieth century, man filled with God's Spirit. The paradox of sacifice. The complexities of freedom. The confusion of our present societies. Your story's happenings should point to a large theme if they are to be significant.

Your writing will be more valid if you present both sides of reality: free grace and also its cost; the beauty of nature as well as its cruelty; selfishness as well as love; confidence as well as despair; the evil of present social structures but also the warmth of human communities.

Birth, death, love, money—the great crises of life— are favorite story themes because they touch the profundity of life at its core. Do not be afraid of writing about violence. A death or two will add drama and heighten interest.

A story speaks of ultimate things through particulars, the universal in the ordinary. Your characters should be both unique and typical of mankind. Your story is to be a slice of life.

6.   WHERE TO WRITE?

After polishing the final paragraph of your manuscript, you do not shove it into a drawer to be eaten by cockroaches. No, you publish it. You pour your ideas into the world.

How do you set this process in motion? Where can you publish?

Here is a list of some Christian magazines and publishing houses in Asia—your potential markets.

BANGLADESH

Bible & Leadership Training
  Program of Sylhet
(Norwegian Mission Board)
Mission House
P.O. Kajaldhara, Dt. Sylhet
Bangladesh

Bible Lit. Centre of the Assoc.
  of Baptists
7 Rashik Hazari Lane
Chawk Bazar
GPO Box 78
Chittagong, Bangladesh

Christian Literature Centre
P.O.Box3, Chandpur
Dt. Comilla, Bangladesh

Every Home Contact
P.O. Box 286
Dacca 2, Bangladesh

HONG KONG

Asian Outreach Ltd.
Commerciai Bldg., 15/f
1 Sugar St., Causeway Bldg.
GPO Box 3448
Hong Kong

Christian Communications Ltd.
Yen Yee Mansion,3/f
29-33 Soarcs Avc.
P.O.Box 95364Tsimshatsui
Kowloon, Hong Kong

Christian Literature Crusade
Kowloon, Hong Kong

Breakthrough
55 Ngau Tau Kok Rd.
Lee Kee Bldg., 1st floor
Block A
Kowloon, Hongkong

Tao Sheng Publishing House
50 A Waterloo Road
Kowloon, Hong Kong

The Alliance Press
31 Chatham Rd.,5/f, Flat C
P.O. Box 95105 Tsimshatsui
Kowloon, Hong Kong

Scripture Union

St. Andrew's Christian Centre,
3/f
138 Nathan Road
Kowloon, Hong kong

The Baptist Press
322 Prince Edward Road
Kowloon, Hong Kong

Seed Press
House141 Prince Edward Rd.,11fl,
Flat H. P.O.Box K-2442
Kowloon Central, Kowloon
Hong Kong

Tien Dao Publishing
151 King's Rd.
Tee Koo Choy Bldg., 2/f B,
P.O.Box 32995 King's Rd.
North Point, Hong Kong

INDIA

Christian Publishing House
7/182 Court Rd.,
Anantapu r 515001
Andhra Pradesh, India

Light of Life Magazine
21 Club Back Road
Byculla, Bombay 8
P.O.Box 4576, Bombay
India

Discipleship Centre
A 42-44 Commercial Complex
Dr. Mukerjee Nagar, Delhi 110 009
GPO Box 1229, Delhi 110 006
India

Masihi Sahitya Sanstha
70 Janpath
New Delhi 110 001
India

Evangelical Literature Society
56 Mosque Road, Fraser Town
Bangalore, India

TRACI Community Theological
Research and Communic. Inst.
TRACI House/Library
105 Savitri Bldg.,
Greater Kailashll
New Delhi 110048, India

Gospel Literature Service
Udyog Bhavan, 250-D
Worli, Bombay 400 025
India

Word of Life Publications
31 Guru Nanak Nagar
Poona 411 002, India

Jiwan Jyoti Prakash
Darjeeling, India

INDONESIA

Gereja Jemaat Kristus Inc.
P. O . Box 73
Bandung, Indonesia

Malachi Evangelistic Assoc.
J I L R E
Martadinata 75
Bandung, Indonesia

Gereja Kristen Kalam Kudus
Jl. Kemayoran Baru 21
Surabaya, Indonesia

Kalam Hidup Publishers
Jl Naripan 67
P.O.Box 156
Bandung, Indonesia

Lembaga Literature Baptis
Jl Tamansari 16
Kotak Pos 56
Bandung, Indonesia

LEPKI—World Vision of Indonesia
Tromol Pos
3532 Jakarta Pusat
Indonesia

OMF Publishers
Jl Letjen Suprapto 28
Cempaka Putih
Jakarta Pusat, Indonesia

Penerbit Gandum Mas
Kotak Pos 46
Malang, Indonesia

YAKIN (Christian Literature
Crusade)
Jl Genteng Besar 85
Surabaya, Indonesia

Yayasan Keluarga &ngkakala
Jalan iman Bonjol 210
Tromol Pos 262
Semanarng, Indonesia

JAPAN

Christian Literature Crusade
1) 4-13-34 Honcho, Higashi
   Kurume Shi, Tokyo 180-03,
   Japan

2) 2-1 Kanda, Surugadai
   Chiyoda-ku, Tokyo 101
   Japan

Japan Mission
6-1 Habikino 1-chome
Habikino Shi, Osaka Fu 583,
Japan

Japan Sunday School Union
9-34 Ishigami 1-chome
Niiza Shi, Saitama Ken 352,
Japan

New Life League
(Shinsei Undo)
1-9-34 Ishigami, Niiza Shi
Saitama Ken, 352 Japan

Word of Life Press
6 Shinanomachi, Shinjuku ku
Tokyo 1 60   Japan

World Outreach Inc.
1-26-2 Minami Sakurazuka
Toyonaka Shi 560, Japan

KOREA

Christian Literature Crusade
CPO Box 103
Dong Dae Mun
Seoul, Korea

Korea Inland Mission
P.O . Box 3
Suwon 120, Korea

Every Home Crusade
P. O. Box 251
Gwang Wha Moon
Seoul, Korea

Word of Life Press & Bible
Book House
Chong Ro Ku
Shin Mood Ro, 1 Ga 58
Seoul 100, Korea

MALAYSIA

Scripture Union
386 Jalan 5/59 Petaling Gardens
Petaling Jaya
Selangor, Malaysia

PAKISTAN

Masihi Isha'at Khana
36 Ferozepur Road
P.O.Box 641
Lahore, Pakistan

PHILIPPINES

Action International Ministries-
-Christ for Greater Manila
92 Shaw Blvd.
Metro Manila
P.O. Box 110
Greenhills, Rizal 3113
Metro Manila, Philippines

OMF Publishers
P.O.Box 2217
Manila, Philippines

Philippine Baptist Mission
2444 Taft Ave.
Manila, Philippines

Alliance Publishers, Inc.
3 West Capitol Drive
 Pasig, Metro Manila
 MCCP.O.Box 1119
Makati, Metro Manila, Philippines

Scripture Union
2123 URC Bldg. Espana
Metro Manila

SRI LANKA

Pragna Publishers
204 Galle Road
Colombo 4, Sri Lanka

TAIWAN

Campus Fellowship Press
22 Roosevelt Road, Sec. 4
P.O.Box 13-144
Taipei, Taiwan

Cosmic Light Inc.
Heen Sheng S. Rd., Sec. 2
Lane 35. No. 7
P.O.Box 1-142
Taipei, Taiwan

China Sunday School Association
105 Chung Shen Road, Sec., 2
P.O.Box 17-116
Taipei, 104, Taiwan

THAILAND

Christian Literature Crusade
487 Silom Road
GPO Box 1050
Bangkok, Thailand

Kanok Bannasan (OMF
Publishers)
135 Pan Road, Silom
Bangkok 10500, Thailand

Full Gospel Publishers
10-12 Sukumvit Road, Soi=6
c/o P.O.Box 11-1116
Bangkok,11 Thailand

Thailand Baptist Mission
90 Soi 2 Sukumvit Road
Box 832
Bangkok, Thailand

To this list you should add other markets as you be come acquainted with them.[1]

Large Christian magazines operate professionally and pay for manuscripts. Smaller ones operate more casually and cannot afford writers' fees in their budgets. Christian publishing houses generally pay something for manuscripts of books, booklets, tracts, et cetera. If you are a beginning writer, you should be happy to start publishing anywhere, even in markets that do not pay. They can be your training ground.

But don't forget secular publications—newspapers, youth magazines, women's magazines, idea magazines, and publishing houses.

McCandlish Philllips, a top reported for The New York Times, has written, "The policy of Satan is the suppression of God's work. The method by which this strategy is conducted is an extreme segregation of Christians away from nearly all the vital centers of power and influence in the nation. The main target is the public consciousness. That is what God wants Christians to reach with the truth, and that is what Satan wants to influence by anything and everything but the truth.

"The publications in the mass public realm—newspapers and magazines that reach many millions of people every day, or every week, or every month—are to an overwhelming degree filled with evil things new excesses in fashion, new excesses in morals, new extremes in occultism and false mysticism, and, of course, much of the current vogue in disruption, violence, and revolution.

"We believers reach ourselves with the truth—and I'm glad that we do—but we allow the mass public media to go the devil's way for want of a few purposeful, faith-filled Christians to occupy them, not for their personal gain, but for Christ . . . .

"The mass media which have daily access to the pubic consciousness are not something wisely to be left entirely in the hands of unbelievers!"[2]

What could you write that would interest a non-Christian editor?

Try some seasonal articles.

At Christmas and Easter, for example, a periodical is obliged to publish something in recognition of the holidays. How bored the staff is with the stale ideas they usually have to dust off. If you could describe how local evangelicals are celebrating these days in unique and significant ways, and could weave in the historical/biblical background for the holiday, many periodicals might find your piece a refreshing change.

Even non-Christian events may be spring-boards. A Christian view of love and sex may sell just before Valentine's Day. A Christian view of death may be in demand during a season when dead ancestors are honored. A Christian view of the nature of man may appeal to an editor when street riots are too disrupting.

Secular publications don't want sermons, but they do want articles on important aspects of life and will often accept such articles from a Christian point of view, if well written.

Since magazines plan far ahead, seasonal articles must be submitted to them several months in advance.

Right now you should learn the difference between news and feature articles. In a news story, the most important facts appear in the first paragraph. Each succeeding paragraph is less important than the one above it. A news story tells who, what, where, when, and how an event happened. It does not use dialogue or illustrations, but quotes authorities and men-on-the-scene. Sentences and paragraphs must be short, and words must be plain and straight forward. There is no place for "pretty" writing. A news story tries to be objective, and does not argue for any position. It focuses on a happening, not an idea.

A **feature,** on the other hand, is an article in which you may take a distinct position or argue for an idea. You have more stylistic freedom than in a news story.

Most articles in newspapers are news, and most articles in magazines are features.

It is important to publish Christian news so that your countrymen will be kept aware that evangelicals are doing something. However, your extensive presentations of a Christian viewpoint must be through features, because it is only here that you are free to explore ideas at length.

Beyond articles, you can introduce Christian thinking into the "public consciousness" through letters-to-the-editor. Relate these to current controversies. For example, you might respond to an article on free love or witchcraft or react to a big business decision that will exploit the working man. Although you will not be paid for letters, this is a worthwhile ministry. And it will train you to write succinctly while applying Christian principles to the nitty-gritty problems of life.

Short pieces may also be published as paid advertisements in magazines or newspapers. In the Philippines, many people respond to this kind of literature evangelism. You will need a sponsoring organization to pay for the ads.

Of course if you have enough money you don't need to go through a publishing house or editor to produce your work. Just take the piece to any printer, arrange the cost and layout design with him, check with him periodically during the printing process, and pay for and pick up your finished product. Then, since you have not worked with any publishing house, you must do all the selling and distributing yourself.

Usually this is not good stewardship of a writer's talents. If you are a writer, you should be freed to write. Furthermore, a publishing house helps with more than the business side: an editor's criticisms may be invaluable aids to improving your writing. Many a famous writer's work has continually improved because he has been supervised by a sympathetic editor. Psychologically, too, there are benefits. Editors who have produced your work will be more likely to encourage and advise you when you are frustrated later. They may well become your co-workers, supporting you with their confidence and counsel. In the lonely work of writing, we need such professional friends. And—they may commission you when they need a special writing job done!

Beyond the publishing house, pray that someone may be called to be a midwife to writers. He can help the writer set up a schedule with deadlines for a given piece of work. He can check back with the writer at each deadline and encourage rather than berate him. He can negotiate with a publisher on the writer's behalf. He can pray with the writer. This job requires a heart for media, writers, and audiences more than it requires copy editing skills. In many cases, we do not so much lack skilled writers as we lack Christian publishers who are willing to spend time in the risky business of nurturing an unknown, who are willing to gamble on a creative thinker who might possibly offend someone somewhere. Credible volunteer agents can bridge that gap between writer and publisher.

But occasionally you may not be able to sell a valuable piece of work. The editors may be too cautious. Or they may not know the grassroots situation like you do. Or those who control the funds may disagree with your view point. What do you do then?

Find a business-minded Christian friend who knows how to raise and manage money. Convince him of the strategic importance of your piece, and persuade him to manage its financing. If he has capital or can raise it, business acumen, and know-how in sales, he can probably make a profit (which, for some reason, is sure to tantalize a businessman!) Asian Christian students sometimes divide the work between those gifted in writing and those gifted in business. In the Philippines, for example, Christian students raised money for an evangelistic newspaper by sponsoring the film "The Gospel According to Saint Matthew" in a downtown theater.

If money remains a barrier, consider mimeographing. When your piece deals with something that Christians want to learn or non-Christians are really perplexed about, they will buy it in spite of its plain look. Call it a "manifesto of the common man"—capitalize on its rugged appearance—and hold your head high you have got your message out in spite of the obstacle of no money.

There are still more markets. Many Christian organizations would like to broadcast an hour on radio or TV once a week—but they lack script writers. Others are broadcasting now, but need fresher, more relevant writing.

You can also write songs with contemporary swing and a Christian message. Or collaborate with an artist to create Christian comics or cartoons. These can have a highly effective ministry, even in the secular press.

Submitting Your Writing to the Publisher

How do you choose among these markets? And how can you find out whether a given market suits your article or book?

Analyze the market you have in mind. Find out what topics and what viewpoints it features. Try to picture the kind of reader it caters to. Careful analyses of several issues of a magazine, for example, can teach you a great deal about whether this market is suitable for your article. Experienced writers never stop studying their markets.

Or visit or write to the publishers. Tell him you would like to write for him. Ask him what writing styles and topics he wants, who his typical reader is, and what he pays.

When you have chosen a market, prepare your manuscript. Type it, double-spaced, with a carbon. If typing is impossible, write it neatly and clearly. Use only one side of sheet of paper.

At the top left hand corner, type your name and address and the date. At the top right hand corner, type the approximate number of words. (You can find this out by counting the number of words in each line for three representative lines, averaging them, and multiplying your average-number-of-words per-line by the number of lines in the manuscript.)

Place your title low on the page—about ten lines beneath your name and address. This leaves room for the editors to write instructions about your manuscript at the top. A few lines under your title, write your name or pen name. Several lines under that, begin your first paragraph.

On the left at the top of each following page, put your family name, a dash, and the main word or words from your title. Put the page number on the right side.

Place your manuscript in an envelope. A used envelope will do: just paste a paper over the side that has been written on, and use the new surface.

Including a "cover sheet" is worthwhile. Here you give the editor a quick glimpse of your article. You present its most appealing aspects—how new the facts are, how many people are affected, why this subject is important. Also you tell the editor why you are qualified to speak about this—either because of the sources you have consulted, or because of your personal background. Make your note brief but compelling.

If the mail service in your country is efficient, it is a good idea to include a plain envelope and stamps inside your package. This is so that the editor will return the article to you if he decides not to use it.

Well-focused action photos to illustrate your piece are invaluable selling aids, if you can get them. Number them on the back, and on an accompanying sheet of paper type "cut lines"—the sentences that will appear under each photo in the publication—corresponding with each number. You may want to put light cardboard into your envelope to protect the photos from bending.

When you submit your piece, by hand or by mail, your stomach will be churning wlth anticipation, and you will ache to know the editor's reaction immediately. You had better start researching and writing something else: it will probably be several months before the publisher makes up his mind about your article!

Selling Your Writing to the Publisher

After a month or two, phone, write, or visit the editor to find out his inital reaction. He may say that your article is being reviewed by a number of editors, or that it is scheduled to be considered by a committee. Be patient. But, in a month, press your inquiries again. Keep this up until you get a definite decision.

Hopefully the decision will be positive and your ideas will be in print. If the publisher has a policy of payment, make sure that you get paid. Some publishers forget this magazines usually pay by the word. Book royalties to the author are about five or ten per cent of the retail price, paid at the end of each year. Publishers often have a standard price for tract manuscripts.

The publisher has the right to select the illustrations, and to do radical stylistic editing, including deletions and additions. But if the meaning is significantly changed, he is obligated to consult you.

The publisher has all the rights and responsiblities in sales and distribution, though the author usually receives a few free copies.

When you sell a manuscript, you sell certain rights. You should find out what rights the editor usually buys (he may be so unaccustomed to dealing with freelance writers that he has no idea!) and should think about what rights you want to sell. You can sell "all rights" or you can sell "first rights." "First rights" means that after the article is printed you can sell "second rights" to another publisher or print the same article. You can limit the publisher's rights to one country or to Asia, or to a limited group of languages or to one language, or to a certain time period, or to a single edition.

On your side, you must respect the publisher's rights. You cannot submit an article to more than one publisher at a time, unless they are in different countries or regions or language groups and you are offering rights limited just to each area or language. And once an article has been bought, it does not belong to you anymore, except outside the area covered by the publisher's rights.

For a book, it is worthwhile to draw up a contract with your prospective publisher.

Obviously, successful freelance writing demands sound management. One essential element is a records and filing system. For example, you might keep each article in a separate large brown envelope. On the outside write the name of the publishing house to which the article has been submitted, and the date of submission. Next, record each visit to or letter from the editor, with its date and result. If the article is accepted, note that, as well as the date and the pay.

If the article is rejected, sometimes the editor will explain why. Weigh his criticisms. Then you may—or may not—rewrite the article before sending it on to the next publisher. Of course you write down the new submission, and its date, on the outside of the envelope. Letters concerning this article, research data, and a copy of the final publication(s) are all filed inside the folder. Small articles are grouped together in one envelope. I keep a numbered list of all the folders, and file them by number. I also keep a list of all articles currently out to publishers.

When you begin to make money through your writing, you may need to keep a financial record for income tax purposes. Find out what writing expenses you can deduct. These may include office supplies, mailing costs, photography costs, salaries for typists or researchers, cost of a room if you use it just for writing, travel, depreciation of equipment like a tape recorder or camera, books and reference materials, et cetera.

Writing involves you in business. You are a steward of information, talent, and time. You must market your work efficiently if you are to maximize your ministry.

---

1 A useful list of U.S. Christian markets has been published in a book entitled *Christian Writers Handbook and Market Guide,* and may be ordered from the Christian Writers Institute. Gundersen Drive and Schmale Road Wheaton. Illinois 60187 USA for two dollars.

2   These quotes are taken from Mr Phillps' lecture at the twenty-
third convention of the Evangelical Press Association in Chicago,
U.S.A., which has since been published in the November, 1971
issue of the *Biola Broadcaster.*

7.   WRITING EXERCISES

1.   Describe a place where you have been afraid (pp. 43-44).

2.   Describe a place where someone has been angry (pp. 43-44).

3.   Take an essay of yours, or an article from a magazine, and change all the verbs you can, using strong and fresh words (p. 43).

4.   Write strong one-page beginnings for three articles (p. 45).

5.   Outline three articles (pp. 45-46,47-49)

6.   Take an essay of yours, or a magazine article, and re-write a few paragraphs as simply as you can (p. 42).

7.   Imagine that a mother has died. The day following her funeral, create a dialogue between:
A. The 28-year old son, who is a lawyer in the city, has married a city girl, and has not lived in the village for years.
B. The 22-year old daughter, who has married a farmer in a nearby village and who has given birth to her first son six months ago.
C. The 8-year old son.
D. The woman who has been her neighbor for many years
E. The woman who employed her as a washerwoman (pp. 49-50).

8.   Imagine that a progressive community development worker has arrived at a village. Create a dialogue between (1) him, (2) a traditional village elder and (3) a young Marxist student who was raised in the village (pp. 49-50).

9.   Sit in a public place (market, restaurant or coffee shop, church,etc.). Listen to people talking. Notice different individuals' speaking styles. Jot down snatches of phrases which show these differences. Later, using these notes, write a dialogue in which characters can be distinguished by their different speech styles (pp. 49-50).

10.   Return to your public place, and make notes of sights, smells, sounds, physical feelings (p. 43).

11.   Return to your public place. Regarding the activities here, find out: Who? What? When? Where? Why?

12. Return to your public place. Ask yourself: What are the significant social groupings here? In each group, are there special ways of dressing? Talking? Behaving? Who are the leaders? What are the other roles? What behavior is appropriate to each role? In each group, are there special celebrations, parties, or rituals? Special reputation associated with the group? Group models, or group villains? (pp. 49-50).

13. Take three Bible characters who have impressed you, and rewrite their stories in contemporary terms(pp. 1-3).

14. List (or draw a picture of) 25 interesting things that you have experienced or seen (pp. 36-41)

15. List (or draw a picture of) 20 of the most significant issues facing your society (pp. 12,30,35-41).

16. Select one local value (honoring parents; redistributing wealth to kin; accumulating wealth as a corporate kin group; a popular sport; etc). Realizing that culture is created by people who are both sinners and in the image of God,
    A. In what particular ways does this value stand under the judgment of God, according to our understanding of the biblical message? Specifically where must we reject it?
    B. In what particular ways is this value part of God's good gifts which he has given us to enjoy richly?
    C. In so far as this value is good, how can we use it creatively—in our individual interaction in society, in our families, in our church organization and activities, in our individual and corporate witness, in our corporate Christian social action? (pp. 33)

17. Write a short, interesting testimony, clearly confronting the points where your people are most likely to misinterpret the gospel (pp. 28).

18. Draw a picture of your dreams for yourself ten years from now (Chap. 2).

19. Draw a picture of your dreams for your national church ten years from now (Chap. 1,p. 3).

20. Circle the metaphors (symbolic phrases) in the following poem. Then develop some metaphors of your own (pp. 43-49).

Mary's Song

Blue homespun and the bend of my breast
keep warm this small hot naked star
fallen to myarms. (Rest . . .
you who have had so far
to come.) Now nearness satisfies
the body of God sweetly. Quiet he lies
whose vigor hurled
a universe. He sleeps
whose eyelids have not closed before.

His breath (so slight it seems
no breath at all) once ruffled the dark deeps
to sprout a world.
Charmed by doves' voices, the whisper of straw,
he dreams,
hearing no music from his other spheres.

Breath, mouth, ears, eyes
he is curtailed
who overflowed all skies,
all years.
Older than eternity, now he
is new. Now native to earth as I am, nailed
to my poor planet, caught that I might be free,
blind in my womb to know my darkness ended,
brought to this birth
for me to be new-born,
and for him to see me mended
I must see him torn. [1]

Luci Shaw

21. Select one magazine. By skimming through several issues, try to find out about it in these areas:

Publisher: Title
               Purpose
               Circulation
               Staff positions
               Editorial policies (if any known)
               Payment to authors
               Non-magazine activities
               Chief competitors

Publication:
    Regular departments
    Kinds of articles (contents)
    Kinds of articles (style)
    Style peculiarities (titles, subtitles,
       beginnings, endings, many or few
       illustrations, formal or informal language,
       etc.)
    Kinds of illustrations
    Kinds of ads
    General appearance (paper, type
       faces, color, size, margins, design
       peculiarities)

Readers:
    Age, other special classifications
    Ideological position (religious,
       political, etc)
    How much money and time, and how
       they prefer to spend these
    Who influences their decisions
    What other media they use
    Values
    Felt needs

22 Interview someone, following these rules, which were developed by Glenn Arnold in *Wnting Award Winning Articles:*[2]

1. **Techniques of Interviewing**
   A. Prepare for the interview
      1. Do your homework
      2. Outline questions
      3. Prepare your attitde
      4. Dress appropriately

   B. 1. Choose a private setting when possible
      2. Make interviewee comfortable
      3. If taping, have machines ready
      4. Establish good rapport
      5. Explain who you are and give interviewee a copy of the publication you represent.

   C. Do the interview
      1. Start with easy questions
      2. Keep control, lisen carefully but don't edit
      3. Use standard English
      4. Avoid questions that can be answered "yes" or "no"
      5. Don't waste time, but don't rush

6. Conclude on an optimistic note
7. Don't promise to publish interview

D. Get photos
   1. Interviewee may have photo he wants to use
   2. Have photographer on hand.

11. Editing the Interview

A. Secure an accurate transcript
B. Decide how you can best use material
   1. Consider slant needed for your publication
   2. Arrange material in order and form desired
   3. Consolidate information on one subject and delete repetitions
   4. Put in transitions
   5. If you keep an interview form, don't be afraid to rearrange questions
C. If advisable, send copy to interviewee for approval
   (PP.44-45)

23. Interview a research librarian to find out what library reference work or what community agency might offer this kind of information:
   book review index
   quote index
   biography index
   indexes to articles in specific fields (i.e., *Social Science Index, Religion Index, General Science Index, Applied Science and Technology Index)*
   geographical and statistical information—almanacs, statistical yearbooks, government departments
   directory of government departments
   current events indexes, such as *Facts on file,* or *Public Affairs Information Service*
   how to research a topic in the back issues of a news paper
   (pp 44-45)

24. Imagine that you are in charge of a publishing program in your country. You would want to have a balanced variety of publications—not too much doctrine and too few biographies, for example. You would want materials that would strengthen the national Church at its weak spots. You would want to promote the kinds of publications that local people like to read.

A. What categories of content should you have?
B. What are the strengths and weaknesses of your national Church?
C. In light of these strengths and weaknesses, which categories of content should you emphasize?
D. What do your people like to read (consider both style and

content)?
E. How can you put the materials they need into forms they will like?
F. How can you distribute your publications most effectively? (pp 30-41)

---

1   Luci Shaw, *Listen* to the *Green,* Wheaton, Illinois, Harold Shaw Publishers, 1971
2   Glen Arnold, *Writing Award Winning Articles,*Thomas Nelson Publishers. Nashville,Tennessee, 1979.